TINY TALKS

A Year of Children's Sermons

VOLUME 1

by Dr. Tony Long

TINY TALKS

A Year of Children's Sermons

VOLUME 1

ISBN-10: 1470149168

ISBN-13: 978-1470149161

ABOUT THE AUTHOR

Tony Long is currently the pastor of CrossWay Baptist Church, Murfreesboro, TN. He has also served as Minister of Education at various churches in TN, TX, and AL. He is a graduate of the University of TN, Southwestern Baptist Theological Seminary and Luther Rice Seminary. He is married to Barbara, has two daughters and five grandchildren.

ABOUT THE BOOK

"Every Sunday, I invite all of the children who are present in the worship service to come to the front, gather around me, and listen to a brief lesson geared specifically to them. And every week leading up to that Sunday, I find myself scrambling to find such a lesson. Maybe you scramble sometimes, too."

"This book is a compilation of a year of ideas that have worked for me. If you've ever tried to find something to share with children, these ideas might help. I call my children's sermon time 'BTBC' *(Brother Tony's Briefcase)*. You may have a much better name. I stole this idea from a visiting evangelist I knew years ago, who used it to generate enthusiasm for each evening's attendance."

"I hand out a preprinted 'BTBC Buck' to each child who comes down for the lesson. These are small dollar bill–sized slips of green paper that say on it 'BTBC Buck.' Then, once every six weeks or so, we have a BTBC Store where they can 'spend' their bucks on inexpensive items like candy, games, gifts for others, etc., anything a child might like. These items are purchased at any inexpensive place I can find. The cost incurred is worth it, because the kids really look forward to their special time in each service."

Tony Long

SUNDAY 1

Needed: Sale ads from the newspaper
Text: John 3:16

"Sorting through this morning's newspaper, I found these ads. Here's one for a sale at Sears. Here's another one from a grocery store, that is selling all kinds of things, edible and non-edible. Here's one advertising nice suits, shirts, and ties. How about this one for a new 50" plasma screen TV? And how about this one, advertising how you can win an X-Box for your house?"

"What if there was in today's newspaper an ad saying that every person who brings two children with them into "Toys'R'Us" before noon today can take home anything in the store for free? What do you think would happen? There wasn't an ad like that, so don't leave. But if there had been, I predict there would be a mass exodus from church right now, with everyone taking two of their best friends with them to "Toys'R'Us."

"Here's today's point. As good as that kind of news would be, we have a better story to tell. It's the story of Jesus' love for everyone. A free toy is great news, but a home in heaven is better news. When Jesus died on the Cross, He made it possible for anyone who trusts Him as their Savior to spend forever in heaven. Read John 3:16. That is the best news that the world could ever hear."

Prayer: *"Thank you, God, for loving us this much. Help us all to get excited about sharing this wonderful news with our friends."*

NOTES

SUNDAY 2

Needed: Hand Mirror
Text: 2 Corinthians 3:18a

"What is this? It's a mirror. When you look into a mirror, what are you expecting to see? You expect to see yourself. But is what you see the real you? No, it's just a reflection of the real you."

"The Bible talks a lot about reflections. Read 2 Corinthians 3:18a. This means that when people look at us, they ought to see a reflection of Jesus. They ought to see by the way we live that we have trusted in Jesus. They ought to be able to tell by the things we say and do that Jesus has changed our lives."

"Sometimes, we look in the mirror and see dirt on our faces. Sometimes, all we can see is the dirt there. That can happen sometimes when we try to reflect Jesus too. They will look at us and not be able to see Jesus at all."

"What are some things that can mess up our reflection? Here are a few things: bad words, hitting people, not reading our Bibles or praying, not going to church. When people see these things present in our lives, they can't see Jesus. It is a very sad thing when these kinds of things are in our lives. We are to be a reflection of the Lord, so that our friends look at us and see Jesus."

Prayer: *"Thank you, God, for boys and girls whose lives show others that Jesus has changed them. Help us to be a reflection of Jesus."*

NOTES

SUNDAY 3

Needed: Halloween masks
Text: Matthew 23:27

"Boys and girls, I want you to close your eyes for a minute. *(Put on one of the masks)* Now open them. Who do you see? What about now? *(Change masks)* What about this one? *(Change masks again)* I am this monster when I put this mask on, but I'm this other one when I put on the other mask. But who am I really? I'm still Brother Tony, no matter which mask it is. On the inside, I will always be Brother Tony."

"Jesus had something to say about wearing masks, and He didn't think that it was a good thing. Read Matthew 23:27. Here, He is talking to some people who were faking who they were. He accused them of pretending to be something that they weren't. He described them as 'being like whitewashed tombs, beautiful on the outside but dead on the inside."

"Are we ever guilty of that, of seeming to be one way on the outside, but being really another way on the inside? Sometimes we can be. If we act like we love Jesus on the outside, when we really don't on the inside, we are just like them. We are what the Bible calls hypocrites. A hypocrite can never please God."

Prayer: *"Thank You, God, that so many of these boys and girls have a clean inside, because they have asked Jesus to come into their hearts. Help us to be genuine, and to not put on masks."*

NOTES

SUNDAY 4

Needed: 1 clean cup, 1 cup painted like dirt on the inside, one bottle of water

Text: Matthew 23:25

"I have a little experiment this morning. Lanny, take this cup. Nicholas, take this other cup. Let me put a little water in each one. Now drink it. Lanny, what's the matter? Why won't you drink it? *(The cup is dirty on the inside)* Show both of the cups to the other children. Here's why Lanny wouldn't drink water from this cup. It looks dirty inside. It's not really, but I wouldn't want to drink out of it either. Both of the cups look alike on the outside, but they are very different on the inside."

"One day, some very religious men came to Jesus. They looked very nice on the outside. They were especially clean, because they thought that God would not be pleased with anything dirty. But their hearts weren't right with God. They had never asked Jesus to be their Savior and Lord. Jesus said that people can be like these two cups. They can look clean on the outside, but not be clean on the inside. Read Matthew 23:25."

"That's a good lesson for all of us. We should be more concerned with keeping ourselves clean on the inside than we are keeping clean on the outside. There should be no room inside for bad thoughts, anger, hatred, things like that. We should want to do the things that please God."

Prayer: *"Dear God, help us to see people for what they are on the inside. Help us to never judge others until we see their hearts."*

NOTES

SUNDAY 5

Needed: Bottle of water
Text: John 4:13-14

"What is this I have in the briefcase today? It's a simple bottle of water. A couple of weeks ago, my family and I went to Disney World in Orlando. We knew that it was going to be hot, and we were going to get thirsty. So we took bottles of water with us, which they would let you do. The night before, we froze one bottle so we would always have cold water to drink. What we didn't know was how quickly we would go through it. When we ran out, we had to buy more."

"They think a lot of their water at Disney World. I could have bought a whole case at home for what one bottle cost there. By the time the day was over, we could have paid for the whole trip. But when your body gets thirsty, you have to have something to drink, no matter what it costs."

"Á woman came to where Jesus was one day, and started to fill up her bucket with some water. Listen to what He said to her. Read John 4:13-14. What He was saying was that, just like we can't live physically without physical water, we can't live spiritually without spiritual water. We can't live like God wants us to live unless we have Jesus in our hearts. And once He comes in, He is there forever. He is our spiritual water."

Prayer: *Thank You, God, that we can satisfy our spiritual thirst for You by inviting Jesus into our hearts. Don't let anyone leave this morning without knowing Christ Jesus personally."*

NOTES

SUNDAY 6

Needed: Camera
Text: Ephesians 5:21

"When you go to Disney World, there is one thing that you do not want to forget to take. You want to make sure that you have a camera. The places you see are incredible, and you'll want to take a picture of those. But you will especially want to take a picture of Mickey and Minnie and Donald and Pluto and all of the rest of the characters. They are dressed up and are roaming the streets of the Magic Kingdom. They are so popular that you have to stand in line just for a picture. In fact, you have to wait in line for just about everything."

"Waiting in line for something is not pleasant. Usually, we want what we want right now. You can forget that at Disney World. But the Bible tells us how to wait in line. Read Ephesians 5:21."

"Submitting means that we put the needs of others before our own. You can't just go to the front of the line. Someone is ahead of you and you have to submit to them before you can move forward. It says we are to submit 'out of reverence for Christ.' By putting their needs first, we will be happier and more content while our own needs are being met."

Prayer: *"Lord, show us how to not want our own way all of the time. Teach us how to submit to the needs of others. Help us to put the needs of others before our own."*

NOTES

SUNDAY 7

Needed: Cell Phone
Text: Mark 12:29-31

"Look what I have for us this morning. It's something some of you might even have. I am almost assured that your mom and dad have one. What is it? It's a cell phone."

"There was a day when cell phones were simple. They just made phone calls. They're not so simple today. Today's cell phone is like a miniature computer."

"Some phones have a camera in it so we can take pictures. I can use my phone to check my emails. Some of them have something called an mp3 player so I can listen to my favorite music. I can actually watch TV on my phone now. They are a lot more complicated now than when they used to just make phone calls."

"It's the same thing in our spiritual lives. People try to make being a God-follower and a Jesus disciple far too complicated. Jesus summed up what it means with these words. Read Mark 12:29-31. The people Jesus was talking to had come up with all kinds of little things that we had to do to please God. Jesus narrowed it down to two: 'Love God and love others.' We should never make it more complicated than that."

Prayer: *"Forgive us, God, when we make following You so complicated. Help us to simply fall in love with You, and show our love for You by the good way we treat others in return."*

NOTES

SUNDAY 8

Needed: Rolls of quarters
Text: Matthew 6:24

"The briefcase this morning is heavier than normal. It's because it's filled with money. What is this? It's rolls of coins, quarters to be exact. I have underneath my sink four cups. Every evening I put my pocket change in those cups, pennies, nickels, dimes, and quarters. Every so often, usually when there is a sports event on TV, I will get out the cups, and put my change into rolls like these."

"The Bible talks a lot about money. In fact, there are more verses that talk about money than there are that talk about heaven. Read Matthew 6:24."

"Jesus knows that how we handle our money shows what we think about God. When money is too important to us, it means that God is not as important as He should be. Loving money is not bad, as long as you use your money to help other boys and girls know better who Jesus is."

"This morning, I want to give each of you a quarter. I want you to decide today how you can use your quarter to point someone to Jesus. You have a big choice to make: Spend your quarter on yourself or spend it on someone else. I look forward to hearing how you spent yours."

Prayer: *"Dear God, thank you for the money we have. We know that all good things come from You. Help these children to be wise in deciding how they will use their money to point their friends to Jesus."*

NOTES

SUNDAY 9

Needed: Picture of someone sticking out their tongue
Text: Proverbs 25:11

"This is a funny looking picture. It's a picture of someone making a funny face by sticking out their tongue. The tongue by itself is a strange thing. It's just a muscle attached to the mouth, but it is very important to the body. We use our tongues for lots of things. We use it to taste our food. We use it to swallow our food after we chew it. Eating would be difficult if we didn't have a tongue."

"One of the most important uses of the tongue is when we talk. I want you to try something. Look at your mom and dad, then grab hold of your tongue and try to say 'lollypop.' You can't do it, can you? What comes out doesn't sound at all like 'lollypop."

"Sometimes, the words that come out of our mouths aren't at all what we mean for them to say. When that happens, we say that we have been 'misunderstood.' Sometimes it's just being mean. Read Proverbs 25:11."

"Aptly spoken' just means that you thought about what you said before you actually said it. Your words weren't hateful, and they certainly weren't bad words. You spoke them like God wants them to be spoken, with love and understanding and thoughtfulness. Our words should always kind words that point people to God."

Prayer: *"Dear God, help our words to always be encouraging and uplifting. Help us to always speak in ways that honor You."*

NOTES

SUNDAY 10

Needed: Tube of toothpaste, toothbrush
Text: Proverbs 8:7

"I reached into my bathroom drawer this morning, and guess what was the first thing I saw? It wasn't a comb (I'm bald). It was a tube of toothpaste lying there with my toothbrush. I'm like many of you. I brush my teeth every morning before I leave the house, and every night before I go to bed."

"Toothpaste comes in all shapes and sizes today. It's not always in a tube like this. It can even come in different flavors. In fact, I don't think there is a standard flavor. You can get cinnamon, or mint, and even some with mouthwash in it. Some containers even have sparkles in them, that I guess are supposed to make you want to use it more often."

"If I were to give you this tube, and ask you to put some of it on the toothbrush, could you do it? Sure you could. That's how it's supposed to be used. If, though, I said that I had made a mistake and asked you to put the toothpaste back in the tube, could you do it? Probably not. Once it's out of the tube, there is no getting it back in."

"Our words are like that. Once we say them, they seldom can be taken back. That why it's so important to be careful what we say. Read Proverbs 8:7. To please God, our words should always be truthful and never be bad."

Prayer: *"God, help us to always be careful with what we say. Help us to always speak the truth, and to never let a lie that we cannot take back come out of our mouth."*

NOTES

SUNDAY 11

Needed: Wrapped present, preprinted slips of paper
(see below)
Text: Matthew 2:11

"Everyone knows what this is. It's a present. Everyone I know likes to get something like this. We enjoy getting presents. A present is a sign that someone has thought about us and loves us. We get them on special occasions, like birthdays. And we give them on special occasions, like Mother's Day or Father's Day. Husbands and wives give and receive gifts on anniversaries."

"When did the giving and receiving of gifts begin? Many people think it began with the wise men. Read Matthew 2:11. Because they loved Jesus, when they finally saw Him, they presented Him with gifts."

"You don't have to have money to give someone a gift. In fact, some of the most special gifts are those that don't cost money. On the slip of paper you have are these words:
Dear <u>(their name)</u>, Because I love God and you very much, I am giving you, every day for one month *(check one, or several, of these)*
❑ my hands to make my bed everyday
❑ my hands to wash the dirty dishes in the sink
❑ my mouth to answer the phone for you
❑ my eyes to clean the bathroom mirror
Signed <u>(your name)</u>

Prayer: *"Dear God, take my gift and use it to show someone how much that I love You."*

NOTES

SUNDAY 12

Needed: Offering envelope
Text: 2 Corinthians 9:7

"Something that nearly all of us scramble to find each Sunday morning is the Offering Envelope. When I was growing up in church, we would hand out boxes of offering envelopes, one envelope for every Sunday of the year, one box per person. Some churches still do that. Others provide them Sunday by Sunday, either in the seats or at the Welcome Center. Some churches today are even using on-line giving. Technology is making it easy to give on-line."

"On the envelope, there is usually a space where you can say what the offering is to be used for. You can designate it for the church's General Fund, which we recommend, or to missions, or to the Building Fund, or to any special event that you wish. All you have to do is tell us what it's for, and we will make sure it is used for that. All of that is on most Offering Envelopes."

"God loves it when His children give generously and when they give cheerfully. That's what the Bible says. Read 2 Corinthians 9:7. He wants our offerings to be given with forethought and out of love. The tithe that the Bible talks about means that we give 10% of what we earn. God promises to generously bless those who give the tithe. It is an expression of worship."

Prayer: *"Dear God, help us to be givers and not just takers. And help us to give cheerfully and generously, always grateful for what You have given us."*

NOTES

SUNDAY 13

Needed: Flyswatter, paddle, switch
Text: Ephesians 6:1-2

"Look at what I found today. A flyswatter, and a paddle, and a switch. These all have one thing in common. They were weapons in the hands of my mother when I was growing up. I would call them the very first 'weapons of mass destruction.' They would all raise little red whelps on my legs when I needed a little attitude adjustment back then."

"None of these things were designed to be used for discipline purposes. But moms and dads sometimes use them to get our attention, don't they? By using them appropriately, they can teach us the difference between right and wrong."

"The Bible has something to say about obeying our parents. Read Ephesians 6:1-2. This verse gives instruction to two groups of people, children and parents. Parents have the responsibility to know what is right when they are trying to teach us. And children have the responsibility of obeying those parents."

"The goal of a good parent is not to hurt us. Their goal is to help us become the best we can be in life. The last part of the verse says that if we will honor and obey our parents, we will live a long life. It's amazing that I am still here."

Prayer: *"Thank You, God, for being our Heavenly Father, and for disciplining us sometimes spiritually. We know that You are trying to help us become the best we can be."*

NOTES

SUNDAY 14

Needed: Floppy disk, CD, memory stick, Bible
Text: 2 Timothy 2:15

"Who knows what this is? It's an old floppy disk for my computer. When they were first created, it amazed people how many computer files they could hold. But then someone got smarter and invented this, a CD. They say a CD will hold the same information as a hundred of the floppy disks. Then they got even smarter and came up with this, something called a removable storage device, or a 'stick," which will hold hundreds of CD's."

"If, however, you want to know about God, where do you go? You go to the Bible. The Bible holds more information about God than you could ever find just on a computer. God's Word is filled with instructions on how to live, and how we can be happy. It tells us how to get to heaven. A computer may hold all of the Bible's words, but no computer by itself can tell us how to obey God. We have to learn that on our own."

"Listen to this verse. Read 2 Timothy 2:15. Boys and girls, to survive in this world, you've got to know the truths found in the Bible. And not only know them, but handle them correctly by obeying them."

Prayer: *"Dear God, teach these boys and girls that life begins and ends with You. And in between, they need to learn everything they can about You. Help them to fall in love with their Bible and to take the time to read it every chance they get while growing up."*

NOTES

SUNDAY 15

Needed: Bible bookmarks that say "Jesus Loves Me"
Text: John 9:15

"I have two of these for each of you this morning (bookmarks). It says on it 'Jesus Loves Me.' I'm giving you two for a reason. I want you to keep one for yourself, but I want you to give the other one to a friend who doesn't go to church anywhere. When you hand it to that person, you can tell them that you go to church where you learn about all the ways that Jesus shows His love to us, and that you would like for them to come with you sometime. That's called witnessing."

"One day, Jesus gave sight to a man who had been born blind. The whole story is in John 9. When asked how he could now see, the man said this. Read John 9:15. He didn't understand exactly how Jesus had done it, but he witnessed to those religious men who were questioning him by telling them what Jesus had done. It was like giving them one of his bookmarks. He challenged them to come and see Jesus for themselves."

"Tomorrow you will see lots of your friends at school. Some of them never go to church. Maybe it's because no one has ever asked them. By giving them a bookmark, you will be asking them to come with you. That's being a witness."

Prayer: "Thank You, God, for opportunities to tell others about You. Use these little bookmarks in ways that we can't even imagine, moving other boys and girls, moms and dads, to come and see what God can do."

NOTES

SUNDAY 16

Needed: Backpack, several large rocks
Text: Psalm 120:2

"I need someone to help me. Here put on this backpack. Now walk over there and back. It's easy, isn't it? Now, put a rock in the backpack. Now walk over there and back. Put another heavy rock in it. It just keeps getting harder, doesn't it?"

"What do you think this verse means? Read Psalm 120:2. The psalmist is warning us to be careful about what we say. Is telling a lie a good thing or a bad thing? It's bad. And the more we tell, the worse things get. One lie always leads to another, and they make life more and more miserable. It's like adding rocks to our backpack. The more we tell, the heavier things become, and the more God is unhappy with us."

"Take the rocks back out. Now try walking. It's easy to walk straight when there are no heavy rocks to carry around. It's just like it's much easier to live right when we tell the truth all the time. Do you think God is happy when we tell lies? No, He is much happier when we tell the truth. It's not a good feeling, is it, when we're weighted down with lies."

Prayer: *"Heavenly Father, thank you for these boys and girls who are learning to tell the truth all of the time. Help all of us, moms and dads, adults and teenagers, to learn the importance of truthfulness. We want to be good children in Your eyes."*

NOTES

SUNDAY 17

Needed: A real motorcycle helmet, a plastic motorcycle helmet that just looks real

Text: Matthew 23:27-28

"Last week, I took off a couple of days, and I did something I don't get to do very often. Jeff, our bass guitar player, and I took a little trip on our motorcycles. We saw some incredibly beautiful country sides, and miles and miles of curvy roads. But before we could leave, we had to put on one of these *(Put on the real helmet)*. We wore helmets just in case we had a wreck and hit our heads on something. Wearing a helmet protected us. And besides, it's the law."

"I knew that my head would be protected because inside my helmet is a tag that reads 'DOT Approved.' This other helmet *(Show the plastic one)* doesn't have a tag like that. It looks like a real helmet, but what if I hit my head really hard while wearing it? I would probably get hurt. It's because it has no protection built in. It just looks real."

"Jesus had something to say about just looking real. Read Matthew 23:27-28. He's saying that we can look like a Christian on the outside, but not be one on the inside. We can do all of the right things, but for the wrong reasons. Jesus doesn't want us to just look good. He wants our hearts to be right."

Prayer: *"Heavenly Father, thank You that we can be genuine on the inside. Forgive us when we are more worried about what others think of us than what You think of us. Help these children to have a faith in Jesus that is real."*

NOTES

SUNDAY 18

Needed: Pair of yard work gloves, golf glove, #1 foam finger glove

Text: John 15:5

"What are these? They are work gloves, the kind someone would use in the yard. They keep your hands warm and clean. Here's one that I like, a golf glove. I wear it when I play golf. It helps me to grip the club better so that I can hopefully hit it farther. Here's the one I really like *(hold up the #1 finger)*. Maybe I can wear this truthfully one day when my favorite team is doing really well."

"Watch this. 'Work glove, I command you to go pull weeds in my flowerbed.' Nothing. 'Golf glove, I command you to 'grip it and rip it.' Nothing. 'Ok, big foam finger, shake yourself and show everyone who your favorite team is.' Again, nothing. Why don't these gloves get up and do what I tell them? It's because they need a hand. They have to have a hand in them before they can do anything."

"The Christian life is just like that. Read John 15:5. In the Christian life, we can't do anything that God wants us to do to honor Him unless we allow Him to live inside of us and to do those things through us. Only with God's help can we live a God-like life."

Prayer: *"Dear God, thank You for the potential that these children have to change the world, if they will allow You to fill their lives with Your presence. Help us all to be like gloves that are filled with Your power to do what You tell us to do."*

NOTES

SUNDAY 19

Needed: Several watches, cell phone with a clock
Text: Matthew 24:44

"What are these? They are watches, all kinds of watches. We have a lot of these at my house, especially in my wife's jewelry drawer. The watch that she wears that day has to be the one that matches the clothes she's wearing. I don't wear a watch much anymore. When I want to know what time it is, I pull out my cell phone. It is supposed to always be right."

"These watches are not always right, and they're certainly not all the same. Even now, one says 9:37, but this one says 9:36. Here's one that says 9:38, while this one reads 9:34. This can be confusing, can't it? Can someone please tell me what time it is?"

"Jesus advised His followers to not worry about the time. Read Matthew 24:44. *'It doesn't do any good to worry about when I am coming again,'* He said *'because no one will be expecting Me when I do.'* Right below this verse, Jesus says that what is important is to be found doing good when He does return, not in an effort to earn our way into heaven, but to show the world that our faith is real. We should be ready, whenever He decides to come back. When that time is will be God's decision to make."

Prayer: *"Dear God, teach these children the importance of doing good deeds. Teach us all that we should worry less about the hour of His return than we do about being found busy doing good things when He does."*

NOTES

SUNDAY 20

Needed: Bottle of disinfectant, rags
Text: 1 John 1:9

"What do I have this morning? Your mom knows what this is. It's what is under nearly every sink. I have a bottle of disinfectant and a rag. I got it out from under our kitchen sink."

"We hear occasionally about a school being closed on account of illness. So many in those schools are sick that they decide to close it for a few days to clean it real good and to let the children get well. Sometimes, whatever it is hits the teachers too. The whole school has to be wiped down with disinfectant. Germs are not good for you. They can be really bad, and they can even kill you if you don't get rid of them."

"The Bible talks about a germ that is really bad. It's the germ called SIN. If it ever gets into your system, it has the potential of killing a person spiritually. It doesn't have to though."

"The Bible tells us how to deal with sin when it pops up in our lives. Read 1 John 1:9. You admit that you've sinned, and that sin destroys a person's fellowship with God. Then you tell God that you're sorry and that you will try your best to not do that sin anymore. That's what it means to confess"

Prayer: *"God, as your children, help us not to disappoint You by sinning. Help us to have the courage to confess the seriousness of sin, and to do our best to avoid it at all costs."*

NOTES

SUNDAY 21

Needed: Name tags (clip-on or magnetic)
Text: Revelation 21:27

"I have in the briefcase this morning something you see a lot of in our church. These are name tags. This one has a little magnet on it that keeps it from falling off. We have lots of people who wear name tags, and have even made one for every Sunday School teacher. Everyone likes to have his name known. And it helps me when everyone has on a name tag, because I am terrible about remembering names."

"The Bible says that there is coming a time when everyone will want their name called. Read Revelation 21:27. I don't know exactly what that book is going to look like. And I don't know if it will be written in pencil, with a pen, or with something we haven't even thought of yet. I'll just leave that up to God. I just want to be sure that my name is written in it. And it is, the moment you trust Jesus as your Savior."

"Boys and girls, the most important decision you will ever make is when you ask Jesus to come into your heart. When you trust in Him and what He did on the Cross for you, He comes into your heart and life. Everyone in heaven will know who you are, because your name, once and for always, will be written down in the Lamb's book of life."

Prayer: *"Dear God, thank You that we can know for sure that our name is written in the book, whatever that book looks like. Help these children to come to a time in their life, if they haven't done so already, when they will ask Jesus to come into their hearts."*

NOTES

SUNDAY 22

Needed: TV remote
Text: Matthew 5:16

"I'll bet all of you know what this is. It's my TV remote. You can't have it. I don't trust anyone with my remote. Yesterday, as we were just waking up, my wife asked me *'Honey, do you have any plans for today?'* I said *'No, nothing before 1:30pm, and nothing after about 4:00pm.'* My favorite team was going to be playing yesterday afternoon and I wanted to watch the game. I could have just listened to it on the radio, and there was a time when I would turn the TV down and the radio up because I loved our announcer. But I wanted to see that game. So yesterday, about 1:30pm, I picked up this remote, hit the ON button, and settled into the Lazy Boy to watch the big game."

"Jesus said that His children should do everything possible to be seen. Read Matthew 5:16. People out there in the world need to see what God is doing. The best way for them to see that is to watch us. They need to see that Jesus makes a difference in our lives. Our good deeds need to shine. That's the best way for people to know that God is real."

Prayer: *"Heavenly Father, thank You that You make a difference in our lives. Thank You for the power to resist temptation. Thank You for strength when we find ourselves weak. Thank you for wisdom when we are confused about a decision we need to make. Let our good deeds shine before others so that they will come to You."*

NOTES

SUNDAY 23

Needed: Large river rock, piece of 2x4
Text: Psalm 18:2

"What do you think they call this? It's not just a rock. It's a river rock. Every Saturday, when my favorite team has a home football game, my wife and I go to my dad's cabin on the river, spend the night there, and go to the game the next day. It's not a fancy cabin, but it's clean, and best of all, it's free. So we go there."

"All along the banks of the river are these kinds of rocks. Nearly every cabin there has a wall made out of these rocks. The owners have gathered them up, set them with mortar or concrete in between, and have made a retaining wall out of river rocks. Some of the cabin owners have even made their cabin's foundation out of river rock. They look really nice."

"Why don't they build their foundations out of this *(hold up the 2x4)*? It's because every so often, there's a flood in that valley. If their foundations were made out of 2x4's and not something solid like a rock, the flood would wash the cabin away, and it would end up somewhere in the Mississippi River."

"Read Psalm 18:2. God is called 'our Rock' for a reason. It's because He can be depended on when life overruns us, when things get really hard, and He will keep us strong when disaster strikes. It is a good thing that God is like a Rock."

Prayer: *"Thank You, God, for always being there when times get hard. Help these children to learn to depend on You in those times."*

NOTES

SUNDAY 24

Needed: Solid mask to hold in front of my face
Text: John 21:7

"If I were to walk down the street with this mask on, would you know it was me? Probably not. With a solid mask over my face, I could be anyone. What if you knew that when I go out to eat at a restaurant, I always ask the waiter or waitress if there is anything I can pray with him about, and that I always leave at least a 25% tip? If you saw that happening, would you automatically know it was Brother Tony? Maybe."

"At our house, we have a rule. When one cooks, the other cleans. Since I don't cook much, I do a lot of cleaning up. The other night, we had about twenty family members over to eat. Since I didn't cook any of it, I got up and just started to load the dishwasher. Once they knew our rule, they knew that it was me doing the cleaning. Without even seeing my face, my actions gave me away."

"That must have been what gave Jesus away. Read John 21:7. It was still early in the morning and probably still dark, but this disciple recognized Jesus by his actions. If someone saw you from a distance, would your actions show that you were a Christian? Without even seeing your face, would your behavior give you away? It should. No one should ever wonder whether or not we've been with God."

Prayer: *"Thank You, Lord, that these boys and girls have the chance every day to show their families and friends that their lives have been changed by Jesus. Give them the wisdom to say and do the things that please You."*

NOTES

SUNDAY 25

Needed: Several loose pennies
Text: Isaiah 12:2

"Listen to the briefcase. It sounds like it's full of marbles, but it's not. It's full of pennies. Let me tell you a story. There was a man who was very wealthy. He invited some friends to go out for dinner. As he was walking into the restaurant, he stopped to pick up a penny he saw lying on the sidewalk. He rubbed it for a moment, put it into his pocket, and went on inside. After a while, his guest commented 'Obviously, you are very wealthy and didn't need that penny. Why then did you stop and pick it up?'

"The man replied 'I know where my blessings in life come from. When I see a coin lying in the street, I pick it up, wipe it off, put it into my pocket, and remind myself that the words on that coin apply to me: In God We Trust. I say to myself right then that trusting in this world doesn't protect you at all. The only thing that really protects a person is his faith in God. I use that coin to remind myself of this."

"The Bible is filled with encouragements to trust in God. Read Isaiah 12:2. Nearly every time God makes Himself known to us in the Bible, He tells us not to be afraid. It's more than just not being scared. It means that, when Jesus is with us, we shouldn't be afraid of anything."

Prayer: *"Heavenly Father, thank You for being the kind of God we can put our trust in. Thank You that You are bigger than any problem or challenge that we might face in life. We trust You to take care of all our needs."*

NOTES

SUNDAY 26

Needed: A Quarter Collection, some foreign coins
Text: Psalm 127:1

"When I was a kid, I collected coins. I had some pretty nice sets, until my little brother decided to punch them out and spend them all. I never have forgiven him for that. In the briefcase today is my most current project. I collected all of the new state quarters. It probably won't be worth much, but I collected them anyway. I have them all."

"Here are some other coins that I have collected through the years. Here are some pesos from Mexico. Here are some that I got while in Romania. They are called lei over there. These coins all look a lot like American money, except for one thing. They don't have those famous four little words on them that ours have: In God We Trust."

"This is one reason I believe that our country is unique. We were founded on a belief in God. They weren't. Those first pilgrims didn't come looking for a beautiful country. They came looking for a land where they could worship God freely and without fear of persecution. There are people today trying to remove God from every part of society. We cannot allow that to happen. Read Psalm 127:1. You cannot build a country without God's help. But with His help, all things are possible."

Prayer: *"Thank You, God, for the privilege of living in the USA. Forgive us for sometimes taking for granted what our country was founded on. Help our country and its leaders to make You proud once again. Let it begin with us."*

NOTES

SUNDAY 27

Needed: Two real Brayburn apples, one artificial apple
Text: 1 Corinthians 3:18

"What are these? They are apples, nice red juicy Brayburn apples, my wife's favorite kind to buy. All of these apples are real, except one. It just looks real. How can you tell the difference? You have to bite it. If it's real, it will be juicy and maybe drip down your chin. You can't bite into the fake one. We have a bowl of these fake ones at our house. My wife loves just seeing them sitting there on the table. They never go bad, and they always look good. But, they are not real."

"Sometimes we fool ourselves into thinking that we are something we are not. God's Word is filled with warnings about doing that. Read 1 Corinthians 3:18. It's telling us here that, when we compare ourselves to the people around us, it's easy to fool ourselves. Instead of looking at others as our standard for living, we should look to God, who never fools anyone. If He is the one we are to please, it just makes sense to live according to His standards, not those of the world."

"Reading the Bible to find out how God wants us to act is the only way we will ever know right from wrong. Have your mommy or daddy read the Bible to you every night before going to bed. You will be so glad when you do."

Prayer: *"Thank You, God, for the Bible that tells us how to act and that helps us not to fool ourselves into thinking we're someone that we're not. Help us to be genuine in Your eyes."*

NOTES

SUNDAY 28

Needed: Baggie of branches from a crape myrtle bush
Text: Matthew 6:31-33

"This is strange to have in the briefcase. It looks like just a bag of sticks, of some kind of branches. I cut them this morning from around the bottom of a crape myrtle bush here at the church. There is a name for those little branches that grow up from the bottom of a crape myrtle, or from the bottom of any bush for that matter. When I was growing up, they were called 'suckers.' They will grow, and will eventually become a limb or branch, but they suck the life out of the rest of the bush. They make the bush look ugly and can actually harm it."

"There are things in life that do the same thing. There are little suckers everywhere that are growing up inside of us. If we don't remove them, they will suck the life out of us and keep us from becoming all that God wants us to become. They usually show up as little bad habits, that start out innocent but grow into something ugly and harmful. Thinking the wrong things, saying bad words, stealing, lying. On and on we could go. Worrying about what we wear and what we eat are big ones today. But these are just suckers in life that need to be cut off. Read Matthew 6:31-33. With God's help, we can remove those suckers."

Pray: *"Thank You, God, for giving us everything we need in life. Forgive us when we worry and fret and get distracted. Help us to remove any of life's suckers that keep us from becoming good children in the Kingdom."*

NOTES

SUNDAY 29

Needed: Flower bouquet in a vase with water, dead
                       flowers
Text: John 4:13-14

"You know what these are. They are fresh cut flowers. My wife loves fresh cut flowers, so we have a lot of them at our house. *(Pull out the dead flowers)* At one time, these were fresh flowers. What's the difference? These are alive, while these others are dead. What keeps flowers alive longer is simple. You water them. Without enough water, even the heartiest flower will die. We all have to have water to live. Without water, we will all shrivel up and die. When you go to the hospital, one of the first things that many doctors do is to give you an IV. He wants to make sure you have plenty of fluids in your system and are not dehydrated."

"It's the same in our spiritual lives. It is possible to look like a fresh bouquet in God's eyes one day, but then dry up and wither away the next. Read John 4:13-14. What kind of water was Jesus talking about? He was talking about the water of life and truth. You can't just drink water once and never drink it again. You have to drink some everyday. You only have to ask Jesus to come into your heart one time. When your faith is genuine, He promises to come in and to never leave. But, to keep us from drying up spiritually, He gives us the Bible to refresh us and to sustain us. He has thought of everything."

Prayer: *"Heavenly Father, help us to realize that Jesus in our heart is like water to flowers. Thank You for always making our lives fresh and beautiful and filled with purpose."*

NOTES

SUNDAY 30

Needed: Trophies, rolls of coins
Text: Philippians 3:14

"This past spring, the local LIONS Club that I'm a member of had its spring fund-raiser. It was a golf tournament. We were raising money to provide glasses and eye surgeries for people who needed them but couldn't afford them. Some of the prizes we offered were trophies like these. Some of the golfers didn't win just a trophy, though. They won money. Golfers like winning money. Some golfers from CrossWay have played in our tournaments."

"The problem with trophies, or money for that case, is that you can't play the sport while holding the prize. The trophies will weigh you down. To play the sport, whether it's golf or football or basketball or anything else, you have to lay down the prize to play it. Everyone wants to be the champion and to win the trophy, but you first have to play the game."

"It's the same with God. Read Philippians 3:14. We should be excited about getting to heaven, life's greatest prize. Heaven is our final goal. But along the way, there are plenty of other prizes to enjoy. We can enjoy the prize of peace, the prize of happiness, the prize of contentment and a life free from worry, and the prize of knowing that all of our needs are being met by God. He promises to give His children all of those things."

Prayer: *"Thank You, Lord, for the prize of heaven. Thank You, also, for the great prizes we get to enjoy along the way there, all because Jesus is in our hearts."*

NOTES

SUNDAY 31

Needed: Pictures of mission trips, missions memorabilia
Text: Matthew 25:40

"On the big screen this morning are pictures we took on our most recent mission trip *(show slides, or hand out pictures. Explain what they are seeing)*. In the yard of one of the houses where we were working was this paddle. No one seemed to know whose it was, so I brought it home as a souvenir of the trip. It reminds me to pray for those who we ministered to while we were there."

"Why do we, as a church, sponsor mission trips? Why do we care if the needs of others are being met or not? We care, because Jesus cares. We had t-shirts printed for our trips that had that sentence on them. Read Matthew 25:40. How many of you would like to do something special for the Lord? I can't imagine anyone not wanting to do that. After all He does for us, we should want to do good things for Him. That verse shows us how we can. It's by doing things for other people in need. That's why we take mission trips. We want to do things for God by meeting the needs of others."

"Kids, one day some of you will want to go with us on a mission trip, if you haven't already. You will learn a lot about yourself, about other people, and about God when you do. It's all because you're busy meeting someone else's needs first."

Prayer: *"Thank You, Lord, for giving us the chance to meet needs, on mission trips and here at home. Help us to do it because we love You."*

NOTES

SUNDAY 32

Needed: Bottles of vitamins, one bottle of multi-vitamins
Text: Ephesians 6:11

"These look like medicines, but they are actually vitamins. I take lots of them every morning. I don't know if they do any good or not. You can look at me and decide for yourself. But I take them anyway. It can't hurt. This one says it promotes a healthy immune function, whatever that means. This one is for the nervous system. If I ever seem a little too nervous on Sundays, obviously I haven't taken enough of those. Some of you could stand a few. And then this one helps me to grow strong bones and teeth. Let me see your teeth. Wow, some coming in, some coming out. Just like some old people this morning."

"But here's one called a 'multi-vitamin.' It has in it a little bit of all of the others. If I had to just take one of these, which one should I pick? That's right, the multi-vitamin. I should pick the one that has a little of all of the others. By taking the others, I'm focusing on just one area, not all of them."

"Read Ephesians 6:11. Paul says we should never just focus on one area. Spiritual warfare touches them all. He says to 'Put on the full armor of God.' We should be able to take our stand for God no matter where we are or what we're doing. Putting on the 'full' armor of God will help us."

Prayer: *"Heavenly Father, thank You that the Bible speaks to every area of life. We don't have to pick and choose. Teach these boys and girls to develop a desire for Your Word that will keep them strong all the days of their lives."*

NOTES

SUNDAY 33

Needed: Medals received from a race
Text: 2 Timothy 4:7

"Let's see if I can show all of these. They are medals you receive on completing a race. You can't buy them. You have to start and finish the race to get one, however long it happens to be. I remember my first ½ marathon, 13.1 miles. I thought I was going to fall over those last three miles. These others weren't much different. Do they give you the medal if you're the fastest runner in the race? No. How about the best dressed runner in the race? Again, no. They give it to you when you cross the finish line and complete the race. You are rewarded for finishing what you started."

"There's a verse in the Bible that talks about finishing the race. Read 2 Timothy 4:7. This is Paul talking. He is in prison, and he could be facing death any day. He is writing to a young preacher named Timothy. As he looks back over his life, he is proud of the fact that he has successfully finished what he had started those many years ago. He says that he has nothing to be ashamed of. That's a great feeling to have."

"So many of you are just getting started in life. When you get to be old, like me, will you be able to say that you've successfully finished what you started? Staying faithful to the Lord is the secret."

Prayer: *"Thank You, God, that You honor faithfulness. Help these children to make a life-long commitment, beginning today, that they will stay faithful to You for the rest of their lives."*

NOTES

SUNDAY 34

Needed: A laptop computer, a memory stick
Text: Galatians 6:7

"I have my laptop computer in the briefcase today. Sometimes, when I'm not in the office, I will take my laptop with me. I use it to work on my sermons mostly. As I finish parts of the sermon, I'll stick this into the side of it, and hit SAVE. Then I can bring my materials back to the office, take the memory stick, and use it to print off what I have saved. It's fairly easy, even for me."

"Let's say that I'm out there, and I write a story about spiders and snakes and monsters and dinosaurs. Scary things. When I hit PRINT, though, I want a story to come out about cakes and ice cream and games and stuff. Fun things. Why don't I get that? Simple, isn't it? You get out of the computer what you have put in to the computer. If I want a happy story to come out, I have to put a happy story in."

"The Bible talks about that. Read Galatians 6:7. If you want good things to happen to you, you have got to do good things for other people. That's one of the laws that governs life. Don't expect God to bless you if you're not busy blessing others. We will reap exactly what we sow in life. And just like the farmer, we will always reap later than we sow and more than we sow."

Prayer: *"Lord God, help these children today to see that what they put into life is what they will get out of life. Help them to give their very best, so that they will in turn receive the very best. All You ask is that we keep You #1 in our lives."*

NOTES

SUNDAY 35

Needed: Sets of old eyeglasses
Text: Ephesians 1:18

"How do I look? How about now? These are some of the eyeglasses that have been donated by some of our members. I'm a member of the LIONS Club. LIONS take old eyeglasses and calibrate them, fix them up, clean them up, and then give them to people who can't see very well. Is this a need? Sure it is. If you wear eyeglasses or contacts, stand up. And I thought I was old. You may be seated. The purpose of glasses is simple: They help you to see better."

"Paul uses the analogy of seeing better when he talks about our relationship with God. Read Ephesians 1:18. God wants us to see better, not just physically but spiritually as well. He wants us to see with spiritual eyes the hope that faith in Jesus gives and all the riches that belong to the children of God. No eyeglasses I've ever seen can help us do that. It takes us seeing with the heart. Some of us need eyeglasses to read our Bibles and our Sunday School lessons. But all of us need glasses on the heart."

"How do we get those kinds of glasses? We get them when we trust Jesus as our Savior. It's like we have put on spiritual glasses. We can, for the first time, begin to understand and appreciate all that God is and all that He does. But it all begins with trusting Jesus as Savior."

Prayer: *"Thank You, God, that the eyes of our hearts can see and understand You better when we trust in Jesus. Help us to see Your love for us and to never doubt."*

NOTES

SUNDAY 36

Needed: Keepsake football with players signatures
Text: John 3:16

"This wouldn't fit in the briefcase. It's a football, but not just an ordinary one. It was given to me by a special lady in the church. It has been signed by all of the members of the team that year. Obviously, none of them could write very well, but here's one player whose name I can read, who is playing in the pro's and doing well."

"If this ball had no signatures on it, it would just be a $30 ball that we would go outside and pass back and forth. But because it has those names, nobody plays with this ball. It stays on a shelf in my office."

"There's a very familiar verse that talks a little about signatures. Read John 3:16. That familiar verse talks about being saved. Whose 'signature' is all over us being saved? I mean, whose idea was this anyway? It was God's idea. Who gave His "only begotten Son"? God did. Who decided that faith in Him, and in Him alone, was always going to be the ticket to eternal life? God did. His signature is all over it."

"It's just like our signed football. It's valuable because of whose signatures are on it. Salvation is valuable because God's signature is on it."

Prayer: *"Dear God, please don't let anyone leave this room today without knowing for certain that they have eternal life. Help us all to know without a doubt that Jesus is in our hearts."*

NOTES

SUNDAY 37

Needed: CD, CDR, CDRW, DVD, DVDR
Text: Ephesians 4:11-12

"I have in the briefcase this morning several CD's. Or at least they all look like CD's. Actually, only this one is a CD. This one is a CDR. This other one is a CDRW. I also have a DVD and a DVDR. You didn't know I knew the difference, did you?"

"We live near Nashville, called Music City USA. You had better know the difference, living near Music City. The point is, while all of these might look alike, they're not alike. They do different things. Our sound guys know, that to try to get one of these to do what only the other one can do, can be very frustrating."

"There's a verse that talks about things looking alike but doing different things. Read Ephesians 4:11-12. Some of us are like this CD. We can preach. Some are CDR's, singers, nursery workers, Sunday School teachers. We might all look kind of alike and dress kind of alike, but we are called to do different things."

"And one other important thing to consider. If that CD couldn't do what a CD is supposed to do, you wouldn't need a CDR or a CDRW. Same in church. If one ministry fails, it affects all of the others. They all fall short. That's how much we need each other to succeed."

Prayer: *"Lord, help us to find our spot in the ministry of this church, and to do that job well. And help us all to learn to work to build each other up."*

NOTES

SUNDAY 38

Needed: 'Smoky' puppet or musical golf head cover
Text: Hebrews 11:6a

"Besides your pastor, who is the #1 University of Tennessee fan? It would have to be this guy, Smoky. Smoky, who roams the sidelines at every UT home game - football, basketball, baseball, it doesn't matter – is the #1 UT fan. Winning or losing, Smoky can always be seen cheering the players on."

"But I want you to picture something in your mind. Pretend that the Smoky costume is just sitting in the locker room. The person who pretends to be Smoky hasn't arrived at the game yet. Can that Smoky costume move? Can it cheer on the team? Can it do anything? The answer is, No. Until that person puts on the costume, all that Smoky can do is sit there. It is impossible for Smoky to do anything."

"Read Hebrews 11:6a. Did you know, without the Lord in your life, it is impossible for you to please God? That's right. People try all the time. They try to be good and try to never do anything wrong. But they can't. They first have to ask Jesus to come into their hearts. Only then do they have any chance of pleasing God."

"Just like Smoky can't move without a person living in him, we can't please God until Jesus lives in us."

Prayer: *"Dear God, help us to show the world that we are Your #1 fan by the things we say and do. Let us open our hearts and ask Jesus to come in today."*

NOTES

SUNDAY 39

Needed: Band-aids for each child
Text: John 9:11

"These are band-aids. Here is one for each one of you. We use band-aids today for all kinds of things. We put band-aids on boo-boo's at my house. Do any of you have a band-aid on a boo-boo this morning? Since becoming a 'poppy,' I carry band-aids in my billfold. Some of mine are plain, but some of them have Snoopy or Garfield on them. I am very popular because of my band-aids."

"Does a band-aid actually heal your boo-boo? Not really. It just hides it while God heals it. A band-aid keeps you from picking at it, until it has time to get better. Jesus made a band-aid one time. Read John 9:11. They didn't have plastic back then, so Jesus' band-aid was made out of mud. The man kept it on his eyes until he could get to the pool to wash it off. When he washed it off, he could see."

"When I had surgery a while ago, the doctor put a big band-aid on my back. It protected the spot where he had cut until it had time to heal. When he finally took the band-aid off, it was all better. I never asked God to make me better, though. I asked Him to keep me faithful, whether it was healed or not. Jesus doesn't heal everyone. I wanted to be a good witness no matter what happened."

Prayer: *"Dear God, thank You that we can be a witness to others, no matter what kinds of boo-boo's we might get. Just like the blind man, help us to give You all of the credit for what You do in our lives."*

NOTES

SUNDAY 40

Needed: Bottled water, bread, a bottle of multi-vitamins
Text: Luke 4:4

"We know what these are – a bottle of water, some bread, and a bottle of vitamins. I take several vitamins every day. I'll bet some of you do, too. I take things like Vitamin C, mainly because it's orange flavored. I take one called B-12, because it's supposed to give you more energy. But one that I always take is this one. It's a daily multi-vitamin, which is supposed to have the daily requirements of several vitamins in it."

"Why do I take vitamins? It's because I can't live just on a diet of these, bread and water. If these were all that I ate every day, I would eventually get sick. My body wouldn't be getting the right amounts of nutrients. My body couldn't fight off all of the germs out there. Vitamins make me stronger and able to resist those germs."

"Jesus said something once that we should all hear. Read Luke 4:4. He was talking to the devil. Jesus was saying that, just like man needs more than just bread to be healthy physically, man also needs more than just the basics to be healthy spiritually. We need the vitamins found in God's Word, the Bible. Saying to the devil 'It is written' shows that even Jesus needed to know what the Bible said."

Prayer: *"Thank You, God, for the special vitamins we find in the Bible that will help us stay strong spiritually. Help these boys and girls to develop a real hunger for the truths that will make them strong."*

NOTES

SUNDAY 41

Needed: A Nicholas Sparks book, a "Left Behind" book
Text: Psalm 119:105

"I try to do a lot of reading. When the 'Left Behind' series of novels were coming out, I could hardly wait for the next one. It was fascinating to me to try to imagine what life will be like after Jesus comes for His church. Those authors stirred my imagination. My wife likes these romance books. They are just fiction, but they are clean and easy to read. I read them too. It takes her about a month to finish one. I read one in about a day and a half. This series of books has little to do with the Lord, but they do make me want to love on my wife a little more."

"But as fun as these kinds of books are to read, they are not my favorite book. Guess what my favorite book is? It's my Bible. Read Psalm 119:105. I read some books about the Bible. Some authors have a great way of making the Bible 'come alive,' so to speak. I like those. But it's not like reading the Bible itself. The Bible tells me everything that I need to know about God. Reading the Bible teaches me how to think, how to talk, and how to act, if I want to please God, which I do."

"If you want to know about God, the Bible is the place to go. If you have learned to read, find a time everyday to read your Bible. If you can't read, have your mom or dad read it to you before you go to sleep at night."

Prayer: *"Dear God, thank You for the Bible. Help us to make knowing what it says a priority in our families."*

NOTES

SUNDAY 42

Needed: Valentines Cards
Text: John 3:16

"Every year when I went to school, I had a girl friend. It wasn't always the same girl, and she didn't always know that I liked her, but every year I had one. I never wondered who I would get a Valentines Card for. Besides one of those 'Greatest Teacher' cards that you always had to give the teacher, I always made sure that one card was more special than all of the others. I usually made it myself."

"Why do we give a really nice card? It's because we think that we love that person. When you love someone, you just want to give them something. It should come naturally. When you love, you want to give. God is like that, too. Read John 3:16. This may be the favorite verse in all of the Bible. Since God loved us, He wanted to give us something special. What He gave us was the most special thing that He had, His only Son."

"God wants us to spend forever with Him in heaven after we die. Jesus' dying on the Cross makes that possible. When He came back to life again, He proved that He could do everything that He had promised. Because of Jesus' death on the Cross, God can offer the gift of heaven. Asking Jesus to come into your heart is the key to guaranteeing that you will go there one day."

Prayer: *"Thank You, God, for loving us and for giving Jesus to us. Help us to love You with all of our hearts, and to show our love for You by loving others."*

NOTES

SUNDAY 43

Needed: Sunglasses, reading glasses, large play
                   glasses
Text: Hebrews 12:2

"We have a box upstairs in our house that has nothing but dress-up clothes in it. It's for the grandbabies when they come to visit. One of the things in the box is these *(Put on the play glasses).* How do I look? In my car, I have something like these *(Put on the sunglasses).* I pretend sometimes that I'm a NASCAR driver when I wear these. But when I'm at home, and I need to read for a long time, I'll put these on *(Put on the reading glasses).* They sit down on the end of my nose, and they make the words in the book bigger and easier to read. I have several pairs."

"The Bible talks about focusing our eyes on the right things. Read Hebrews 12:2. The writer of Hebrews says that, if we want to focus our eyes on something important in life, we should focus them on Jesus. When we see Jesus clearly, we see God clearly. He came to the earth to show us what God is like. To understand God, we have to understand who Jesus is and what Jesus has done for us."

"The most important thing that Jesus has done is to die on the Cross. And He is now sitting next to God, just waiting for the command to come back and take us to be with Him."

Prayer: *"Lord, help these boys and girls to want more than anything to see Jesus clearly. Help them to learn exactly how much Jesus loves them, and what He has done for them so they can go to heaven one day."*

NOTES

SUNDAY 44

Needed: Blank calendar for the coming year
Text: Joshua 1:8

"Here is something right off of my desk. It's a calendar for the coming year. You'll notice that it's nice and blank, at least it is beyond the coming month. Slowly but surely, my calendar will get filled up with my plans and my activities. But it's blank right now. I have a choice to make. What do I decide to fill my calendar with? Some things we have to do, but some things we decide to do. I hope that everything that I eventually write down in my calendar will point people to God. But we have a choice to make."

"One day, God told a man named Joshua what he should fill his calendar with. Read Joshua 1:8. God wanted Joshua to be successful in everything that he did. He was getting ready to lead God's people into the Promised Land. God couldn't afford for Joshua to not be successful. The key to success was learning all he could about the Bible he had, meditating on what he read, and then putting it all into practice. And Joshua needed for God's people to do the same thing."

"Boys and girls, and you who are moms and dads too, the key to our success in life is tied to the Word of God. If we hope to become all that God has planned, we need to learn all we can about the Bible, meditate on it, and put it into practice. It's as simple as that."

Prayer: *"Lord, help us to fill our lives with things that will please You. Help us to hunger for Your Word, and to put into practice what we learn."*

NOTES

SUNDAY 45

Needed: Digital camera, camera charger
Text: Matthew 26:36

"Everyone knows what this is. It's a camera. But you might not know what this is. This is a charger for my camera. When I know I am going to be using my camera for a long time, I always make sure that I charge it the night before. My camera has a battery in it. When I take lots of pictures, the battery gets weak and runs down. But by placing it on the charger, the battery is restored, and I'm ready to take all of the pictures I want to."

"In a way, people have inside them what I call 'spiritual batteries.' They're not real batteries, but every once in a while, we need to 'have our batteries charged.' Our faith can get a little weak, and we just need something to lift us up."

"Jesus was the same way. Read Matthew 26:36. Jesus was getting ready to have to do the hardest thing He would ever do. He was to be our Savior. He was getting ready to show everyone that He loved us so much that He was willing to die on the Cross to pay our sin debt. If He was going to be the Savior that He had declared Himself to be, He needed to make sure that His 'spiritual batteries' were all charged up. So He spent more time praying. It charged His batteries."

Prayer: *"Lord, teach these children the importance of staying in touch with You. Help them to keep their faith strong and fully charged, so that they can be the kind of Christian that You want them to be."*

NOTES

SUNDAY 46

Needed: Folded map
Text: John 14:6

"Some of you have never seen one of these. And I hate to unfold it, because you can never refold one the same way. When I was a kid, every summer we would take a trip somewhere. Most trips would be to Florida to where my grandparents had moved, but every year we would go somewhere. That annual trip was a challenge to my dad. He would pull out his maps and try to plan the best route we could take to get there as fast as possible. Getting there quicker was always the goal."

"Today, we don't use maps like this much. Instead, we 'Google' where we want to go. Google maps are unbelievable. They can get you to where you're going within a foot or two. And the time it will take you to get there? How do they know so much? Many people today have a GPS built right into their car. It's kind of cool to see the road you're on, right there for you to follow."

"If you were going to draw out a map for someone on how to get to heaven, could you do it? Thomas asked Jesus that very question. Read John 14:6. To get to heaven, there is only one way. It's by trusting in Jesus. Just draw a picture of Him hanging on the Cross, with a heart right under it. Jesus in your heart is all a person needs to know."

Prayer: *"Heavenly Father, thank You for making sure that we have the most important map we could ever have. We know how to get to heaven. Thank You for sending us Jesus."*

NOTES

SUNDAY 47

Needed: Hair clippers
Text: John 6:47

"I would bet none of you has any of these. These are my hair trimmers. I used to go to the barbershop and pay a lady $10 to cut my hair. You would think I'd get a discount (bald). I watched her do it, and thought to myself *'Tony, you could do that.'* So I went to the store, bought these clippers, and have been cutting my own hair ever since."

"Do you ever watch the old TV reruns? They had some pretty strange hair styles back then. Most of you don't remember the Beatles, but they helped to bring in long hair and beards. The hippy generation that followed changed hair styles for everyone. Growing up, my daddy would give my brother and me a buzz, long before a buzz was popular. One good buzz would last the whole summer."

"Some churches that I know teach that, to get to heaven, you have to dress a certain way or look a certain way, their way of course. The Bible never says anything about that. Read John 6:47. It doesn't say, 'He who has short hair' or 'He who has long hair.' It doesn't say 'She who wears dresses, or pants, or jeans, or shorts.' It says, 'He who believes.' As long as it's big enough and thick enough to cover everything, God doesn't care. Trusting in Jesus is all that matters."

Prayer: *"Thank You, Lord, for looking at the inside, not the outside. Help us to be more concerned with the heart than we are with the clothes or the hair style. Give us a chance to tell someone about You today."*

NOTES

SUNDAY 48

Needed: Bag of bows
Text: Romans 6:23

"The briefcase today is filled with things we all love seeing. Bows. What usually comes with a bow? A present. I went to a birthday party yesterday for a one-year old. She opened her presents, but I doubt that she remembers any of them. Her big sister, though, who is just a couple of years older, saw all of those packages with bows and just knew that they were all for her. Anything with a bow was fair game. It was a wild party. When we see something with a bow on it, we get excited. It means that a gift is somewhere close by."

"The Bible talks about gifts. Read Romans 6:23. It wouldn't be a gift if you had to do something to earn it. With a gift, you either take it and open it, or you don't. Eternal life in heaven is like that. It is a gift. When Jesus died on that Cross, God could now offer us that gift, which He does. He offers us the gift of eternal life. It's just like a present with your name on it. But you have a choice to make. Take it, or don't take it."

"When I was eleven years old, I reached out and took God's gift. I asked Jesus to come into my heart. I became a child of God's. Once you are His child, you are always His child. You have been born again."

Prayer: *"Lord, thank You for the wonderful gift of eternal life. Thank You that we can know first-hand all about Your love for us. Please, don't let anyone leave this morning without knowing that the gift of everlasting life is theirs."*

NOTES

SUNDAY 49

Needed: Infant-sized cheerleader outfit
Text: Matthew 5:43-44

"I have this morning the cutest little cheerleader outfit. Well, it's almost the cutest. Here's why I have this. I remember when I was in grammar school. There were some kids who were hard to like. In fact, if there ever was an enemy, it was them. They were usually the bigger kids. They had the habit of picking on us little kids, and saying mean things to us. Sometimes I've heard parents tell their children to fight back when that happens. If they get bitten, they should bite back, literally. I don't know how scriptural that advice is."

"This outfit is actually a gift. As you can see, this is for one of Tennessee's opponent's teams. In a sense, they are Tennessee's enemies, at least one Saturday each year. They sometimes do things to TN and say things about TN that aren't nice. But that's what enemies do."

"But Jesus said to not act like that. Read Matthew 5:43-44. When someone treats you meanly, Jesus says to love them in return, not hurt them back. That's a very hard thing to do. To love an enemy is something that you need God's help to do. But it honors Him and proves that your goal is life really is to become like Jesus. Jesus always loved His enemies."

Prayer: *"Dear God, thank You for the example of Jesus. Show us how we should be treating those who may be treating us badly. We want to honor You and we want to show the world that knowing Jesus really does make a difference."*

NOTES

SUNDAY 50

Needed: Bar of soap, wash cloth, deodorant power
Text: 1 John 1:9

"This is a brand of deodorant powder, the kind you usually put on after a shower or bath. The other day, I had been working outside and had gotten hot and sweaty. I wasn't smelling very good. Barbara asked me to go to the store for something. I didn't want to go anywhere smelling, but instead of going in and cleaning up, I went inside, sprinkled on some of this, changed shirts, and to the store I went."

"The question to you is, 'Was I really clean?' or did I just cover up the bad smell?. If I had really cleaned up, I would have taken a shower, and used these, a bar of soap and a wash cloth."

"There's a verse that talks about getting clean in God's eyes. Read 1 John 1:9. In the spiritual world, sinning makes us unclean in God's eyes. A sin is when we do what God says not to do, or don't do what He says we should be doing. Either way, it makes us dirty to God. There is only one thing to do. We have to agree with God that we're wrong, and promise that we will do our best not to let that happen again. That's what it means to confess. If we confess our sins, He promises to make us clean again. A clean child is always better than a dirty one."

Prayer: *"God, thank You that we can be honest with You about our sins. Thank You that You've provided a way we can get ourselves clean in your eyes. Help us to want to stay clean in Your sight."*

NOTES

SUNDAY 51

Needed: A caulk gun, a tube of caulk, paintbrush
Text: Matthew 16:6

"This is a caulk gun. You place a tube of caulk in it, like this, and put the caulk into the cracks you might find in trim work or in woodwork. Recently, our church participated in some mission work, after one of the hurricanes had hit the coast. Since I have a bad back, my job was to fill in the cracks of the trim that was being installed. When the caulk dried, I painted the trim with this *(paintbrush).* And there was lot of it. Every house we saw was damaged."

"I discovered something about trimming and painting. A good trim man is a painter's best friend. When all of the cracks are smooth and all of the corners are neatly done, it's easy to paint. The paint goes on quickly, and the finished job looks very professional. But to be truthful, the caulk and the paint only hide the flaws in the trim. They don't correct them. The cracks are still there."

"Did you know that it's possible to look good on the outside but still be full of cracks on the inside? Read Matthew 16:6. The men called the Pharisees didn't believe that faith in Jesus was enough to get into heaven. They thought you had to earn it by being good. Jesus says that is wrong. They looked good on the outside, but inside they had cracks."

Prayer: *"Dear God, help us to trust only in Jesus to get us to heaven, and to beware of those people who think you have to be good enough. Help us to fall in love with Jesus."*

NOTES

SUNDAY 52

Needed: Pumice stone
Text: Proverb 28:14

"This is called a pumice stone. You can get one at any place that sells bath supplies. It is used to make rough places on your body, like calluses, smooth again. I think they are made from volcano rock. A callous can be a bad thing or a good thing. A callous is a spot on your skin that has gotten hard, usually by rubbing it over and over. The bad calluses, like you can get on your feet sometimes, need a pumice stone to make them smooth and less painful. I always wanted a golfer's callous. That would mean that I was playing a lot of golf. But I don't have one."

"It's possible to get those hard calluses on our hearts. Those are always bad. Hard hearts usually get that way from ignoring God or from messing around with sin. Read Proverb 28:14. When we honor the Lord and do the things He tells us to do, our hearts stay soft. God likes it when our hearts are soft. He does His best work in hearts that are soft and responsive to Him. He can't work in a heart that has become callused or hardened."

"Smoothing out our hard spots is what God does best. The truths in the Bible break them apart, and God's Spirit keeps them soft. Our job in life is to obey Him and to be faithful to Him, no matter what life brings our way."

Prayer: *"Thank You, Lord, that we don't have to have hard hearts. Keep the hearts of these boys and girls soft as they listen to and obey the truths found in Your Word."*

NOTES

Made in the USA
Middletown, DE
24 August 2015